© 2025 Alisa L. Grace
All rights reserved.

No part of this book may be reproduced in any form or by any electronic or mechanical means, including information storage and retrieval systems, without permission in writing from the publisher.

Self-Published by
Alisa L. Grace
Sanford, FL 32771

ISBN: 978-1-966129-13-4

First Edition

Printed in the United States of America

Library of Congress Cataloging-in-Publication Data
Grace, Alisa L.
Title of the Book: Mind Architect: How Your Thoughts Design Your Destiny
Library of Congress Control Number: 2024923770

Disclaimer: The views expressed in this book are those of the author and do not necessarily reflect any organizations or individuals mentioned.

Acknowledgments: The author wishes to thank God, Her Husband (Linion), Victory Temple of God, Florida SPECS, Unity Youth Association, All About Serving You, Angels-ANJ Events, NordeVest, and Love & Create Life for their support and contributions.

This book is dedicated to you, the reader, the dreamer, the one who dares to believe in a brighter future. May the words within these pages ignite a spark of transformation, empowering you to embrace your mind's limitless potential and create a life that radiates joy, purpose, and fulfillment.

Why You Should Read This Book

If you're tired of feeling like life is happening *to* you instead of *for* you, this book is your roadmap to reclaiming control. "Mind Architect" isn't just another self-help book; it's a practical guide to understanding your thoughts' profound impact on your reality. Through a blend of science-backed insights, inspiring stories, and actionable exercises, you'll discover how to break free from limiting beliefs, cultivate a mindset of abundance, and consciously create the life you've always dreamed of. Whether you're seeking more tremendous success, deeper fulfillment, or simply a more joyful existence, this book empowers you to become the architect of your destiny. It's time to stop settling for a life built on autopilot and start designing a masterpiece that reflects the true desires of your heart.

Table of Contents

Introduction 11
   Mind Architect: How Your Thoughts Design Your Destiny 11

Chapter 1: The Power of Thoughts 13
   The Architects of Our Reality 13
   The Mind-Reality Connection: A Symphony of Science and Spirit 13
   The Self-Fulfilling Prophecy: Our Beliefs Become Our Reality 13
   Harnessing the Power of Thought 14
   Transformative Questions 15

Chapter 2: Identifying Limiting Beliefs 17
   The Shadows That Bind 17
   Unveiling Subconscious Programming 17
   Common Limiting Beliefs 18
   Breaking Free from the Shadows 18
   Transformative Questions 19

Chapter 3: The Art of Reframing 21
   Turning Shadows into Light 21
   Challenging Negative Thoughts 21
   Cultivating a Positive Mindset 21
   From Limitation to Liberation 22
   Transformative Questions 23

Chapter 4: Visualization and Affirmations 25
   Painting Your Dreams into Reality 25
   Harnessing the Power of Imagination 25
   Crafting Effective Affirmations 25
   From Vision to Victory 26
   Transformative Questions 27

Chapter 5: Gratitude and Abundance 29
Unlocking the Flow of Blessings 29
Shifting from Scarcity to Abundance 29
Practicing Gratitude Daily 29
The Ripple Effect of Gratitude 30
From Barrenness to Blossoming 30
Transformative Questions 31

Chapter 6: Taking Action 33
From Dreams to Deeds 33
Bridging the Gap Between Thought and Reality 33
Setting Goals and Creating a Plan 33
From Intention to Manifestation 34
Transformative Questions 35

Chapter 7: Overcoming Obstacles 37
Rising Stronger from the Ashes 37
Embracing Challenges as Opportunities 37
Developing Resilience 37
From Setbacks to Stepping Stones 38
Transformative Questions 39

Conclusion 41
The Master Architect of Your Destiny 41
Empowerment and Call to Action 41
Transformative Questions 43

Resources for Further Exploration 45
Additional Resources 45

Meet The Author: Alisa Ladawn Grace 47
Love's Unconditional Revolution! Unleash and Ignite the Transformative Power of Love 47
Other Works by Alisa Ladawn Grace 47
One Gives Life, and One Steals Life 48
Mind Architect: How Your Thoughts Design Your Destiny 48

Mind Architect: How Your Thoughts Design Your Destiny

Introduction

Mind Architect: How Your Thoughts Design Your Destiny

Unleashing the Power Within to Build the Life You Love

Have you ever felt like a passenger in your own life, watching the scenery change but unable to control the destination? Do you find yourself caught in a loop of self-doubt and negativity, unable to break free from the chains of your mind? What if you could rewrite the script, redesign the blueprint, and become the master architect of your reality?

The ancient proverb, "As a man thinketh in his heart, so is he," whispers a profound truth that echoes through the ages. Your thoughts are not simply moving whispers in the wind; they are the architects of your life, shaping your experiences, relationships, and, ultimately, your destiny.

In this transformative journey, we will delve into the extraordinary power of your mind, exploring the profound connection between your thoughts and the reality you create. We will uncover the hidden beliefs and patterns that may hold you back and equip you with the tools to reframe your mindset and unlock your limitless potential.

Prepare to embark on a quest of self-discovery, where you will:

- **Unravel the Mind-Reality Connection:** Understand the science behind how your thoughts shape your world and learn to harness this power for positive change.

- **Identify and Conquer Limiting Beliefs:** Expose the self-sabotaging thoughts that keep you trapped and replace them with empowering affirmations.

- **Master the Art of Reframing:** Transform negative thought patterns into opportunities for growth and cultivate a mindset of abundance and possibility.

- **Visualize and Manifest Your Dreams:** Learn to create a mental blueprint for success and attract your desires into your life.

- **Embrace Gratitude and Abundance:** Shift your perspective from scarcity to abundance and unlock the flow of blessings.

- **Take Inspired Action:** Bridge the gap between thought and reality by aligning your actions with your dreams.

- **Overcome Obstacles with Resilience:** Develop the mental fortitude to navigate challenges and emerge more vital than ever.

This book is your invitation to become the architect of your own life. It's time to break free from the limitations of your past, embrace the power of your present, and design a future that fills your heart with joy and purpose.

Are you ready to unlock your extraordinary potential and create a reality reflecting your desires?

Let's begin.

Chapter 1: The Power of Thoughts

The Architects of Our Reality

In the grand tapestry of life, our thoughts are not mere fleeting threads; they are the master weavers, intricately crafting the patterns and designs that shape our experiences. Science and scripture converge to illuminate the undeniable truth that our thoughts possess extraordinary power, influencing our actions, emotions, and, ultimately, the reality we inhabit.

The Mind-Reality Connection: A Symphony of Science and Spirit

Neuroscience reveals that our brains are constantly abuzz with electrical activity, generating thoughts, emotions, and memories. Like well-trodden trails in a forest, these neural pathways strengthen with repeated use. The more we focus on a particular idea or belief, the more deeply ingrained it becomes in our subconscious.

This phenomenon aligns beautifully with the wisdom found in Proverbs 23:7: "For as he thinketh in his heart, so is he." The thoughts in our conscious and subconscious minds are great ideas planted in the fertile soil of innovation, ready to grow into something extraordinary. They become powerful influences on our lives. With consistent attention and nurturing, these seeds blossom into beliefs, shaping our perception of ourselves and the world around us.

The Self-Fulfilling Prophecy: Our Beliefs Become Our Reality

Consider the power of the placebo effect, where patients experience genuine healing simply by believing they receive adequate treatment. This demonstrates our beliefs' remarkable influence on physical and emotional well-being.

Similarly, the Bible speaks of the power of faith to move mountains (Matthew 17:20). When we unwaveringly believe in a positive outcome, we ignite a reservoir of inner strength and resilience that propels us toward our goals.

Conversely, negative thoughts and self-doubt can become self-fulfilling prophecies. When we dwell on fears and limitations, we create mental barriers that hinder our progress and dim our light. The saying goes, "Whether you think you can or can't, you're right."

Harnessing the Power of Thought

Recognizing the profound link between our thoughts and reality allows us to shape our lives actively. By harnessing the power of our thoughts, we can shape our destinies and manifest the life we desire. Focusing on positive, empowering thoughts cultivates a fertile ground for success, happiness, and fulfillment.

In the upcoming chapters, we will explore practical methods for recognizing and altering limiting beliefs, nurturing a positive mindset, and utilizing visualization and affirmations. As we navigate this voyage of self-discovery, it's essential to remember that your thoughts have a profound impact and serve as the blueprint for your life. Mastering your mentality can create a reality that reflects your deepest desires and highest aspirations. The power to shape your destiny lies within your mind.

Transformative Questions

1. What recurring thoughts or beliefs may be shaping your current reality?

   _____

   _____

   _____

   _____

2. How can you consciously cultivate a more positive and empowering mindset?

   _____

   _____

   _____

   _____

3. In what areas of your life would you like to see transformation, and how can you use the power of your thoughts to achieve those goals?

   _____

   _____

   _____

   _____

Notes:

_____
_____
_____
_____
_____
_____
_____
_____
_____
_____
_____

Chapter 2: Identifying Limiting Beliefs

The Shadows That Bind

Visualize your mind as a rich, expansive landscape filled with endless possibilities, diverse terrains, and undiscovered treasures. Though the outer surface may exude tranquility, beneath it lies a tapestry of deeply rooted beliefs and behaviors shaped by our upbringing and life experiences. These subconscious patterns act as guiding forces, influencing our actions and decisions. Understanding and reshaping these patterns can unleash our full potential and chart a more fulfilling journey. As the Apostle Paul urges us in Romans 12:2, "Do not conform to the pattern of this world but be transformed by the renewing of your mind." This transformative process begins with shining a light on these limiting beliefs, bringing them to the surface where they can be examined and, ultimately, released.

Unveiling Subconscious Programming

Limiting beliefs often operate beneath our conscious awareness, whispering doubts and fears that undermine our confidence and sabotage our efforts. "The power of these beliefs is evident in their ability to manifest in a multitude of compelling ways, including:"

- **Negative self-talk:** "I'm not smart enough," "I'm not attractive enough," "I'll never be successful."

- **Fear of failure:** Avoiding challenges and opportunities for growth due to a fear of not measuring up.

- **Perfectionism** involves setting unattainably high standards and experiencing feelings of disappointment that arise when we encounter inevitable setbacks.

- **People-pleasing:** Prioritizing the needs and opinions of others at the expense of our well-being.

Common Limiting Beliefs

While limiting beliefs are as unique as fingerprints, certain patterns tend to emerge. Some of the most prevalent negative thought patterns include:

- **"I'm not good enough."** This pervasive belief can stem from childhood experiences or comparisons to others, leading to feelings of inadequacy and low self-worth. Remember, you are fearfully and wonderfully made (Psalm 139:14), and your value is inherent, not dependent on external validation.

- **"I'll never succeed."** This belief can paralyze us with fear, preventing us from taking risks and pursuing our dreams. Yet, the Bible reminds us that with God, all things are possible (Matthew 19:26).

- **"I don't deserve happiness."** This belief can stem from a sense of unworthiness or past mistakes, creating a barrier to experiencing joy and fulfillment. However, God's love is unconditional (Romans 8:38-39), and you deserve His blessings.

Breaking Free from the Shadows

Acknowledging these limiting beliefs is the initial step toward liberation. By bringing them into the light of conscious awareness, we can begin to challenge their validity and replace them with empowering truths.

In the next chapter, we will explore the art of reframing, learning how to transform negative thought patterns into positive affirmations that fuel our growth and propel us toward our goals.

Remember, your past or your limitations do not define you. You are a masterpiece in progress, capable of painting a life filled with joy, abundance, and purpose.

Transformative Questions

1. What limiting beliefs may be holding you back from reaching your full potential?

   _____

   _____

   _____

   _____

2. How do these beliefs manifest in your thoughts, emotions, and actions?

   _____

   _____

   _____

   _____

3. Are you ready to challenge these beliefs and embrace a new, empowering narrative for your life?

   _____

   _____

   _____

   _____

Notes:

_____
_____
_____
_____
_____
_____
_____
_____
_____
_____
_____
_____

Chapter 3:
The Art of Reframing

Turning Shadows into Light

Imagine standing before a magnificent stained-glass window, its vibrant colors dancing in the sunlight. Once sharp and fragmented, each piece of glass has been transformed into breathtaking art. Similarly, the art of reframing allows us to take the broken pieces of our limiting beliefs and reassemble them into a masterpiece of empowerment and possibility.

As the Bible reminds us in Ephesians 4:23, "to be made new in the attitude of your minds." This renewal involves a conscious shift in perspective, focusing on the light rather than the shadows. It's about challenging the negative narratives that have held us captive and replacing them with affirmations that uplift and inspire.

Challenging Negative Thoughts

The first step in reframing is to become aware of our negative thought patterns. When you catch yourself thinking, "I'm not good enough," pause and ask yourself:

- **Is this thought true?** What evidence supports or contradicts this belief?
- **Is this thought helpful?** Does it serve me or hinder my progress?
- **Is there a more empowering way to view this situation?** What alternative perspectives can I consider?

By questioning the validity of our negative thoughts, we create space for new possibilities to emerge.

Cultivating a Positive Mindset

Reframing is not about denying challenges or pretending everything is perfect. It's about focusing on the positive aspects of any situation and finding growth opportunities even amid adversity.

Here are some practical techniques for cultivating a positive mindset:

- **Gratitude:** Focus on the blessings in your life, big and small. "Give thanks in all circumstances; for this is God's will for you in Christ Jesus." (1 Thessalonians 5:18)

- **Affirmations:** Repeat positive statements about yourself and your goals. "I can do all this through him who gives me strength." (Philippians 4:13)

- **Visualization:** Imagine yourself achieving your dreams and experiencing success. "Faith is the substance of things hoped for, the evidence of things not seen." (Hebrews 11:1)

- **Surround yourself with positivity:** Spend time with people who uplift and inspire you. "As iron sharpens iron, so one person sharpens another." (Proverbs 27:17)

From Limitation to Liberation

The art of reframing is a powerful tool for transforming our inner world and, consequently, our outer reality. We create fertile ground for growth, abundance, and joy by consciously focusing on empowering thoughts and beliefs.

As you continue on this journey of self-discovery, remember that you can shape your reality through the lens of your thoughts. Embrace the art of reframing, and watch as the shadows of limitation give way to the radiant light of possibility.

Transformative Questions

1. What negative thought patterns do you notice most frequently in your life?

   _____

   _____

   _____

   _____

2. How can these thoughts be transformed into more empowering affirmations?

   _____

   _____

   _____

   _____

3. What positive changes do you envision as you master the art of reframing?

   _____

   _____

   _____

   _____

Notes:

_____
_____
_____
_____
_____
_____
_____
_____
_____
_____
_____

Chapter 4: Visualization and Affirmations

Painting Your Dreams into Reality

Imagine yourself as a painter standing before a blank canvas, a vision taking shape in your mind's eye. Each brush stroke makes the image more apparent, colors blend, and textures emerge until a masterpiece is born. Similarly, visualization and affirmations are the brushstrokes we use to paint our dreams into reality, harnessing the power of imagination and belief to manifest our desires.

Hebrews 11:1 reminds us, "Faith is the substance of things hoped for, the evidence of things not seen." Through visualization and affirmations, we tap into this unseen realm of possibility, creating a mental blueprint for success and attracting desired outcomes into our lives.

Harnessing the Power of Imagination

Visualization is more than just daydreaming; it's a deliberate and focused practice that engages all our senses. By vividly imagining ourselves achieving our goals, we create a powerful mental rehearsal that primes our minds and bodies for success.

Olympic athletes, successful entrepreneurs, and renowned artists all attest to the power of visualization in their journeys. By consistently visualizing their desired outcomes, they masterfully create a sense of familiarity and confidence that translates into real-world accomplishments.

Crafting Effective Affirmations

Affirmations are positive statements that help reinforce our desired beliefs and outcomes. They can reprogram our subconscious mind when repeated regularly, replacing limiting beliefs with empowering truths.

To create effective affirmations, consider the following guidelines:

- **Use the present tense:** "I am confident and capable."
- **Be specific and positive:** "I am attracting abundance and prosperity into my life."
- **Make them personal and meaningful:** "I am living my purpose and positively impacting the world."
- **Repeat them with conviction and emotion:** Feel the truth of your affirmations as you speak them.

From Vision to Victory

Visualization and affirmations are not magic spells; they are tools that work in harmony with the laws of the universe. By aligning our thoughts, beliefs, and actions with our desired outcomes, we create a powerful, energetic field that attracts opportunities and resources to support our goals.

Remember that imagination is a sacred gift as you continue exploring your mind's power. Use it to paint a vivid picture of the life you desire, and let your affirmations be the soundtrack that guides you toward its realization.

Transformative Questions

1. What are your most profound dreams and aspirations? Visualize them in detail, engaging your senses.

   _____

   _____

   _____

   _____

2. What limiting beliefs might be hindering your progress? Craft empowering affirmations to counteract these beliefs.

   _____

   _____

   _____

   _____

3. How can you incorporate visualization and affirmations into your daily routine to manifest your desires?

   _____

   _____

   _____

   _____

Notes:

_____
_____
_____
_____
_____
_____
_____
_____
_____
_____
_____

Chapter 5: Gratitude and Abundance

Unlocking the Flow of Blessings

Imagine two gardens side-by-side. One is arid and barren, its soil cracked and dry, while the other is lush and vibrant, overflowing with blossoms and fruit. The difference? One garden receives the nourishment of gratitude, while a scarcity mindset starves the other.

Gratitude is the fertile soil in which abundance grows. It shifts our focus from what we lack to what we have, opening our hearts and minds to the infinite possibilities surrounding us. 1 Thessalonians 5:18 reminds us, "Give thanks in all circumstances; for this is God's will for you in Christ Jesus." This call to gratitude is not just a suggestion but a divine invitation to experience the fullness of life.

Shifting from Scarcity to Abundance

A scarcity mindset tells us there's not enough to go around - not enough love, money, or opportunities. This mindset creates a sense of fear and competition, leading us to hoard resources and mistrust others.

In contrast, an abundance mindset recognizes the infinite generosity of the universe. It understands that there is enough for everyone and that our blessings are not diminished by sharing them with others. This mindset fosters a sense of gratitude, generosity, and collaboration, opening the floodgates for even greater abundance to flow into our lives.

Practicing Gratitude Daily

Gratitude is not a one-time event; it's a daily practice that nourishes our souls and attracts blessings. Here are some simple yet powerful exercises to cultivate a habit of gratitude:

- **Gratitude Journal:** Write down three things you are grateful for each day. These can be big or small, from a warm cup of coffee to a loving relationship.

- **Gratitude Meditation:** Take a few minutes each day to sit in stillness and focus on the blessings in your life. Feel the warmth of gratitude fill your heart and radiate throughout your body.
- **Gratitude Expressions:** Express your appreciation to others through words, notes, or acts of kindness. "Therefore encourage one another and build each other up, just as you are doing." (1 Thessalonians 5:11)

The Ripple Effect of Gratitude

Gratitude is not only a magnet for abundance; it's also a catalyst for transformation. Focusing on the good in our lives elevates our vibration and attracts more positive experiences.

Moreover, gratitude nurtures a feeling of interconnectedness and compassion. As we recognize our blessings, we are more likely to extend generosity and kindness to others. "Each of you should use whatever gift you have received to serve others, as faithful stewards of God's grace in its various forms." (1 Peter 4:10)

From Barrenness to Blossoming

Gratitude is the key to a life of abundance and fulfillment. Shifting our mindset from a focus on scarcity to one of gratitude opens up fertile ground for our aspirations to not only take root but also thrive and grow.

As you continue your journey of personal transformation, remember that gratitude is not just a feeling; it's a choice. Cultivate gratitude daily and watch your life blossom with blessings beyond measure.

Transformative Questions

1. What are three things you are grateful for today? Take a moment to reflect on these blessings and feel the warmth of gratitude in your heart.

   _____

   _____

   _____

   _____

2. In what areas of your life do you tend to focus on scarcity rather than abundance? How can I adjust my perspective to nurture a mindset of gratitude?

   _____

   _____

   _____

   _____

3. How can you express gratitude to others today? Consider a small act of kindness or a heartfelt message of appreciation.

   _____

   _____

   _____

   _____

Notes:

_____
_____
_____
_____
_____
_____
_____
_____
_____
_____
_____
_____

Chapter 6: Taking Action

From Dreams to Deeds

Imagine a majestic bridge spanning a vast chasm, connecting the realm of dreams to the shores of reality. This bridge is built not with steel and concrete but with the unwavering power of action.

As the Bible reminds us in James 2:20, "Faith without works is dead." Our thoughts and beliefs, no matter how potent, remain fantasies unless accompanied by deliberate and purposeful action. This chapter is your call to bridge the gap between your mental creations and the tangible world, transforming your dreams into deeds.

Bridging the Gap Between Thought and Reality

The mind is a powerful tool, but more is needed to visualize and affirm our desires simply. To manifest our dreams, we must act inspired, aligning our behaviors with our beliefs.

This means:

- **Stepping outside your comfort zone:** Embracing challenges and conquering fears is essential for fueling growth and transformation.

- **Embracing imperfection:** Don't let the pursuit of perfection paralyze you. Take action, even if imperfect, and learn along the way.

- **Persisting through setbacks:** Obstacles are inevitable but don't define us. Use them as opportunities to learn and grow stronger.

Setting Goals and Creating a Plan

A dream without a plan is just a wish. Setting clear, actionable goals is essential to turn your visions into reality.

The SMART goal-setting framework can help you create a roadmap for success:

- **Specific:** Clearly define what you want to achieve.
- **Measurable:** Establish criteria for tracking your progress.
- **Achievable:** Set realistic goals that challenge you but are still attainable.
- **Relevant:** Ensure your goals align with your values and overall vision.
- **Time-bound:** Set deadlines to create a sense of urgency and accountability.

Once goals are defined, breaking them into smaller, actionable steps can make them feel less overwhelming and more manageable. It's important to remember that even the longest journey begins with a single step.

From Intention to Manifestation

Taking action is the bridge that transforms your mental creations into tangible realities. It is the catalyst that brings your dreams to life. As you step onto this bridge, remember that you are not alone. The universe conspires to support those who are aligned with their purpose.

"Commit to the LORD whatever you do, and he will establish your plans." (Proverbs 16:3)

Transformative Questions

1. What actions can you take today to move closer to your goals?

   _____

   _____

   _____

   _____

2. What fears or obstacles are holding you back from taking action? How can you overcome them?

   _____

   _____

   _____

   _____

3. How can you create a plan that aligns your actions with your thoughts and beliefs, leading to the manifestation of your dreams?

   _____

   _____

   _____

   _____

Notes:

_____

_____

_____

_____

_____

_____

_____

_____

_____

_____

Chapter 7: Overcoming Obstacles

Rising Stronger from the Ashes

Life is a winding path with its fair share of twists, turns, and unexpected detours rather than a smooth, paved road. Obstacles, setbacks, and challenges are inevitable but do not define us. They can become the catalysts for our most significant growth and transformation.

The Apostle Paul declared in Philippians 4:13, "I can do all this through him who gives me strength." This unwavering faith in a higher power and a resilient spirit allow us to navigate life's storms and emerge stronger on the other side.

Embracing Challenges as Opportunities

Every challenge presents an opportunity for learning, growth, and self-discovery. Instead of viewing setbacks as failures, we can reframe them as valuable lessons that equip us with the wisdom and resilience needed to succeed in the long run.

Consider the story of Thomas Edison, who famously said, "I have not failed. I've just found 10,000 ways that won't work." Despite countless setbacks, his relentless pursuit of the incandescent light bulb demonstrates the power of perseverance and a positive mindset.

Remember, diamonds are formed under immense pressure. Similarly, our character is forged in the crucible of challenges. Each obstacle we overcome strengthens our resolve and deepens our understanding of ourselves and the world around us.

Developing Resilience

Resilience encompasses the capacity to recover from setbacks, face hardships, and continue to foster optimism in the face of adversity. It involves not shying away from challenges but confronting them with composure, bravery, and steadfast belief in oneself.

Here are some strategies for developing resilience:

- **Cultivate a growth mindset:** See challenges as chances for growth and advancement. "Not only so, but we also glory in our sufferings, because we know that suffering produces perseverance; perseverance, character; and character, hope." (Romans 5:3-4)

- **Practice self-compassion:** Be kind to yourself when you face setbacks. It's important to remember that everyone makes mistakes, and it's acceptable to be imperfect.

- **Seek support:** Don't hesitate to lean on the support of trusted friends, family, or mentors for the encouragement and guidance you need. "Two are better than one, because they have a good return for their labor: If either of them falls, one can help the other up." (Ecclesiastes 4:9-10)

- **Focus on solutions:** Instead of dwelling on problems, channel your energy into finding solutions. "And we know that in all things God works for the good of those who love him, who have been called according to his purpose." (Romans 8:28)

From Setbacks to Stepping Stones

Obstacles are not roadblocks; they are stepping stones to success. By embracing challenges with a resilient spirit and unwavering faith, we can transform setbacks into opportunities for growth and emerge more vital than ever.

Remember, you are not alone on this journey. Draw strength from your faith, community, and unwavering belief in your potential. As you navigate life's challenges, may you find the courage to rise above adversity and create a reality that reflects your resilience and determination.

Transformative Questions

1. What obstacles are you presently encountering, and how can you transform them into opportunities for personal development?

   _____
   _____
   _____
   _____

2. What strategies can you implement to develop greater resilience in adversity?

   _____
   _____
   _____
   _____

3. How can your faith be a source of strength and guidance as you navigate life's obstacles?

   _____
   _____
   _____
   _____

Notes:

_____
_____
_____
_____
_____
_____
_____
_____
_____
_____
_____
_____

Conclusion

The Master Architect of Your Destiny

As we reach the culmination of this transformative journey, let us recap the fundamental principles that have illuminated our path:

- **Your thoughts are the architects of your reality:** The thoughts you cultivate, whether conscious or subconscious, shape your beliefs, actions, and experiences.

- **Limiting beliefs can hold you back:** Identify and reframe these negative thought patterns to unlock your full potential.

- **Visualization and affirmations are powerful tools:** Harness the power of your imagination to create a mental blueprint for success and attract your desires.

- **Gratitude is the fertile soil of abundance:** Cultivate a mindset of gratitude to attract blessings and experience greater joy and fulfillment.

- **Action bridges thought and reality:** Align your actions with your beliefs and take inspired steps toward your goals.

- **Obstacles are growth opportunities:** Embrace challenges with resilience and unwavering faith, emerging more robust from every setback.

Empowerment and Call to Action

You are not a passive observer in the story of your life; you are the author, the director, and the master architect. The power to shape your destiny lies within your mind.

Embrace this truth with courage and conviction. Take ownership of your mentality, cultivate positive thoughts, and align your actions with your dreams.

As 1 Chronicles 22:13 reminds us, "You will be successful if you carefully obey all the decrees and regulations that the LORD gave to Moses for Israel. Be strong and courageous! Do not be afraid or discouraged."

Let these words be your anthem as you step into the fullness of your potential. The world is waiting for your unique gifts and contributions. Go forth and create a life reflecting the beauty, brilliance, and boundless love within you.

Transformative Questions

1. How will you apply the principles from this book to create a more fulfilling and purposeful life?

   _____
   _____
   _____
   _____

2. What actions will you take to cultivate a positive mindset and overcome limiting beliefs?

   _____
   _____
   _____
   _____

3. What legacy do you want to leave in the world, and how can you use the power of your thoughts to achieve it?

   _____
   _____
   _____
   _____

Notes:

_____
_____
_____
_____
_____
_____
_____
_____
_____
_____
_____

Resources for Further Exploration

As you continue mastering your mentality and creating your reality, we encourage you to delve deeper into the fascinating world of thought power and personal transformation. Here are some recommended books that can provide further guidance and inspiration:

1. Switch On Your Brain: The Key to Peak Happiness, Thinking, and Health by Dr. Caroline Leaf

Dr. Leaf's groundbreaking work explores the science behind the mind-brain connection and offers practical tools for managing your thoughts and emotions to achieve optimal well-being.

2. Winning the War in Your Mind: Change Your Thinking, Change Your Life by Craig Groeschel

Pastor Craig Groeschel provides a faith-based perspective on overcoming negative thought patterns and experiencing victory in your mental battles.

3. Battlefield of the Mind: Winning the Battle in Your Mind by Joyce Meyer

Joyce Meyer's classic book offers biblical insights and practical strategies for renewing your mind and overcoming the lies that hold you back.

Additional Resources

- **Podcasts:** Explore podcasts focusing on personal development, mindset, and spirituality.
- **Online Courses:** Consider enrolling in online courses or workshops that teach mindfulness, meditation, and other techniques for mastering your thoughts.
- **Support Groups:** Join forces with fellow travelers on the path to personal growth and transformation.

The journey of self-discovery and personal growth is ongoing. You must proactively seek resources that inspire and empower you. Never doubt your ability to create a life that reflects your deepest desires and highest aspirations.

> **"The mind is everything.**
> **What you think you become."**
> **— Buddha**

Meet The Author: Alisa Ladawn Grace

Alisa Ladawn Grace is a multifaceted individual who embodies a life dedicated to love and service. A retired school administrator, author, transformative life coach, and devoted local missionary, she has spent over 30 years spreading love's transformative power in a world often marked by division and discord.

Alisa's unwavering belief in the power of unconditional love shines through in her writing and her life. She is convinced that love is the ultimate catalyst for change, offering a beacon of hope in even the darkest of times. Her works inspire readers to embrace love's transformative potential and apply it to every aspect of their lives.

Love's Unconditional Revolution! Unleash and Ignite the Transformative Power of Love

In this powerful book, Alisa explores the practical application of the timeless principles of love found in 1 Corinthians 13. Discover how these principles can revolutionize relationships, work, personal growth, and spirituality. Prepare to be amazed at love's profound impact on your life when you intentionally choose to live by its tenets.

Other Works by Alisa Ladawn Grace

Alisa's commitment to nurturing the next generation is evident in her children's books, which promote civic engagement and personal development. Titles like *Civic Heroes: Discovering Elections with the Supervisor of Elections*, *My Civic Adventure: Learning About Voting and Community!*, and *Unlocking Your Great Potential Within You: A Comprehensive Curriculum Guide to Nurturing Children's Meditation, Executive Functioning Skills, and Good Habits* empower young minds to make a positive difference in the world.

One Gives Life, and One Steals Life

Alisa's latest work, *One Gives Life and One Steals Life*, delves into our choices' profound impact on our present lives and the legacy we leave for future generations. Through insightful exploration and a call to action, Alisa encourages readers to choose life by aligning their decisions with God's will and teaching the next generation to do the same. This book is a powerful reminder that our choices matter and that we have the power to create a life-giving legacy that will bless generations to come.

Mind Architect: How Your Thoughts Design Your Destiny

In addition to her other transformative works, Alisa Ladawn Grace invites you on a journey of self-discovery and empowerment with *Mind Architect: How Your Thoughts Design Your Destiny*. This book delves into the profound connection between your thoughts and the reality you create, providing practical tools to harness the power of your mind and manifest the life you desire.

Through her writing and her life, Alisa Ladawn Grace continues to be a shining example of love's transformative power. Her works inspire, uplift, and empower readers to embrace love, make life-giving choices, and create a reality that reflects their deepest desires and highest aspirations.